# LONELY HEARTBREAKS

# VON

# "LONELY HEARTBREAKS"

## :VON

FOR
EVERYONE

# "THE BEGINNING"

## ''''Never Been"

*Never been in love,*
*So what is it?*
*Is it morning sex or holidays*
*with each other's embarrassing*
*families,*
*Is it long walks on a beach*
*Or dinner parties with drunk*
*friends,*
*Is it arguing about nothing or each*
*other's insecurities,*
*Is it forever or just 1,000*
*days*

*A lot of confusion*
*Just to die alone in the end.*

## "Valley Girl"

She used me for a night
To feel like a star without
the lights,
Just to go back to him in
the light,
To make his eggs like he
likes.

## "Nights with her"

You fuck me great every night
I guess you had a lot of practice at a
young age and
That's horrible
If you really ponder the
situation,
Now a bunch of adults with
Trauma
Massing with unhealthy vices
That leave you stuck
But who am I to tell you
How to handle your pain,
When I'm stuck with this death
stick
In my mouth.

## "Zodiac"

*You're nothing more than
pretty
eyes,and long legs
Extra trauma to give you an
excused for your
Shitty ways.*

## "Huh"

Flowers always die eventually
in a vase or from the concrete,
Everything seems pretty complex
But in the end it might be the
simplest thing to understand
You're here
Then you're not
Always enjoy the sun and the gloomy
days.

# "Fathom"

Her body
Makes the angels
jealous,
Zeus can't fathom
Her beauty,
She's wanted by all
For all the wrong
reasons.

## "Summer 2914"

White lines
Or Green,
Nights in a loop
I hope they delete every
Memory of you.

## "Ego's 10:02"

History repeats her self and
everyone gets bored
Of the same ride
They want more drama
To feed their
Ego's
Oversized
Appetite

## "Common"

I'm used to filling my
sorrows with empty holes
and empty bottles
With empty conversations
about
Nothing and you're the common
denominator
between them all.

## "Pack of Cigarettes"

Cigarettes don't keep
me warm like your lies
She said
"Your lies are often like the
ones my father
told my mother to keep her
mouth shut
whenever he arrived home later
than
usual"
And
A response like that deserves
a pack of
cigarettes....

# "Pyramid Stories"

"Her hips move
A certain way to
catch
everyones
Eye but the one she
wants,
She works like a
machine
With no operator,
More in tune but
All alone"

## "Dating"

I might be interested but my wallet
is empty
How do you woo a pretty woman
you never met with empty
pockets and a heart looking for a
connection
Falling in love with pictures
Is a crazy mess,
All I want to do is say
Hello

## "10 Year Reunion"


Don't talk to me about that
Those memories are gone and
forgotten
Drowning at the end of a
empty bottle.

## "12 Steps"

I'm in love with fucking you,
Does it make me evil
To want your body more
Than your mind
Lusting after you is a hell of a
substance
That needs 12 steps of recovery.

## "PC"

Cigarettes never smell
good
not even under
Palm trees
I hope you're doing more.

## "Nothing but"

She's never available
Always in her head,
Nothing but the thoughts of her
existence
And a cigarette in her hand.

## "L - D"

Death is my lover
We dance everyday around the sun
She's really into
My misery
I wonder why
She's not more into me.

## "154"

Nights like this
You play your favorite
playlist,
Too many shuffles to find your
Favorite song..
Shitty weed and cheap liquor
To patch up your fragile feelings,
Hoping 09'
didn't last forever.

## "Fries and Lies"

I miss your curly hair
It reminds me of curly fries and
all your silly lies
You always mess up my
favorite things.

## "Instagram Nights"

Endless scrolling
On adventure-less night
I seen a old friends story with
A new face
With eyes golden like the sun
She caught my eye
A follow for a follow
Every thought I see intrigues
my soul
I would like to know more,
And grow each other's core
Before that though
Another thought shown
You already with the person
that makes you grow.

## "Most things"

Nights likely end with me
Without you
Going through withdrawals
Hoping you'll never call me again
I know it doesn't make sense
Like most things I say.

## "Disaster"

Mentally unfit
To have my love
Bloody noses
And dirty bathrooms,
Is all we have from this lovely
disaster.

# "High watching the menu"

I wish I could inhale a blunt with
you
And don't commit,
Talk about my bullshit
And you respond like a mood ring,
Selfish act by me I must say..
But time will tell I only used you
as a emotional whore.

## "MEMO and MOTTO"

Boredom and lust go together like
fries and burgers
I hope this doesn't go over your
head,
She said
It's more like a memo
To live by
Not a motto
You can break whenever you
want to leave me.

## "Daydreams & You"

Daydreams of you
Are never fun
I never get any work done
Cigarettes and your face is
what all my days are composed of.

## "Dumb"

I'm glad you didn't accept
My heart
Now I can see I was young and dumb
Full of insecurities
That you wouldn't understand.

## "Lovely"

Lovely like a summer night
She's open and ready
For love or maybe
Just a bottle of wine and a lonely
smoke.

"....."


I want to write about you every time
I'm intoxicated
Off expensive
Wine
Which is always
Necessary
When these
Nights are
A little bit more
Silent than the rest.

## "August 4,1994

I hope it doesn't last forever,
Thoughts about you
Hurt
And the only medicine for that
Is a white line of endless
Possibilities.

## "Felt inspired Today"

She's in love with him
but posing
For the world like a model on
The catwalk
With nothing on
But black lingerie & her ego.
Hoping she can still the attention
of the world
Even with him at home.

## "Someone's Pretending"

You kissed my burns
To make me believe it was real
It never was
I was just a side of fries to
Your already oversized meal.

## "BULLSHIT"

Your picture attracts
Many eyes and many likes,
And more messages than you can
handle,
In love with your beauty
They miss your most intriguing
Part.

## "Oscar 2"

Everything with you is
complicated like
All your favorite movies.
You deserve an Oscar
For your performance
You did with this
lonely heart

## "Your Crutch"

Cigarettes
Leftover from the night before
I hope everything's okay
You never leave your crutch
Not even on a rainy day.

## "Confidence"

My life is too complicated to shoot a
shot
To shy to say anything
So I guess I'm stuck liking these
pictures
Of you
Until confidence isn't a issue of
mines.

## "After thought"

I'm an after thought to you
You only want me when you're
Unsober and unruly
You're more complicated
Than physics
How could I ever understand
A math equation from
God.

## "Broken Calls"

I used to care about cracked
phones until you destroyed too
many to count
Now broken glass cuts my
fingers
every time
I reject your calls

## "RED FLAGS"

### Everyone has red flags
Mines aren't that simple
Like yours I struggle too,
Mines is smoking too much weed
On a Monday
Lusting for women's bodies
Like a hungry stomach
That can't get full,
Gluttony of lust..
I call it
Its pretty shameful
I might say but not more shameful
than
Blaming a man that wasn't there
for a kid
For all the problems this man
faces now

So I struggle just like you,
So work on your red flags
And I work on mine too.

Heartbreaks are never sober or fast
Always chaotic and develops character
We don't want
But what are heart needs
Never settle for less than what your
heart deserves
Always love yourself and be gentle
to your heart.

# "THE END"

Made in the USA
Columbia, SC
17 October 2024

44548892R00031